Cooking Italian

By Joe Bianco

From
"My Dear Italian Mother's
Peasant Recipes"

Avellino Press
PO Box 8454
Portland, OR 97202

Cover design by the Benedictine Press
Illustrations by Dean McMullen
ISBN 0-9643408-4-4

contents

how it began . . .

My childhood memories are warm thoughts of stickball, kick-the-can, boxball, hide-and-seek, and the pungent odors of cooking that meant happiness and security to a knicker-clad youth growing up in a mixed neighborhood.

This all took place in Newark, New Jersey, an aging industrial giant situated on the less than verdant shores of the sludgy Passaic River. It was my birthplace, and I fondly refer to it as home, although others less blessed refer to Newark in anything but fond terms.

Ringed by Jersey City, Hoboken and the lesser known communities of Hackensack, Bayonne, and the Oranges, Newark is a veritable garden of gastronomic delight. But the one thing that makes it a special haven for its children is the Italian cooking – more specifically, Neapolitan cooking, and more precisely for me, my dear mother's peasant recipes, brought to these needy shores when the 20th century was in diapers.

What a joy it was to come home after the long Sunday masses in Latin at St. Antoninus to smell those penetrating, easily-identifiable odors coming from the first floor kitchen where my mother performed her culinary magic.

If it was just an "ordinary" Sunday creation we could expect pizzaola and linguine or parmigiana or maybe lasagna with scrumptious meatballs and melted mozzerella or rice or pasta.

But if it was an occasion or a holiday, she would create with her delicate, talented hands, ravioli with riccotta (cheese), chicken alla caccitore, occhi di lupe (large sized macaroni) and braciola.

We would begin with an escarole soup which whetted the appetite and kept you in suspense while waiting for the next carefully planned course. The arrival of each serving was executed in such a manner as to not rush you but not to keep you waiting too long, either. It was the epitome of logistics. My dear Italian mother knew just how much to serve, when to serve, how long to keep you waiting between courses – all designed to control the senses, to keep your focus on one thing: the food that she prepared with orchestrated perfection several hours earlier. How that marvelous Queen of the kitchen managed to blend all those ingredients in a short time without help into a full five-course dinner, is a secret I selfishly tried to steal from her.

"Now Ma," I would say, "How did you make the sauce for the spaghetti?"

"It's nothing. I use a little of this and a little of that."

And so it went. Was I to lose forever the kitchen secrets that had made my childhood a memorable experience of eating pleasure? There was little else in the 30's for a child to remember fondly except those Italian dinners.

Those were stark, lean, unexciting years.

They were years that generated what was to become the holocaust of the century. They were poor, desperate years of little money, no diversion; years of struggle for frightened refugees who wanted greatly to be accepted in a foreign, unfriendly society.

They were hard times for my growing-up years. Patches on knickers; white shirts only on Sunday; Eton hats only for Easter. Five cents for a treat – a small, saucer-size apple pie at Petite's candy store. And then ten cents for the Deluxe movie house on South Orange Avenue where Bela Lugosi toyed with our imagination. Sometimes it was a choice: ten cents for the Deluxe or the apple pie.

"You had enough junk yesterday," my mother would admonish. "You had such a beautiful dinner. Why do you fill your stomach with that terrible junk?"

She knew. What mother didn't know junk food from the real thing? However, apple pies then, more than likely contained wholesome ingredients. Preservatives or artificial foods were not as abundant as today.

But I enjoyed "junk food" once in a while. (What kid didn't?) You got tired of a diet of fresh vegetables, freshly slaughtered chicken, homemade breads and other healthy foods.

I seldom ate between meals; mostly because I couldn't afford it. Seldom were there extra pennies for soft drinks or ice cream. I would splurge on a two-cent plain seltzer and a penny's worth of licorice. But I was addicted to those two cent Hooten bars, a treat to share with a friend who often split the cost.

These are the things I remember of my youth, the formative years when my mother's cooking made such a deep impression on me.

Now, I am going to share recipes of Italian delight, seldom revealed or experienced except, of course, in the kitchen of my dear Italian mother. I have shared some of her dishes with others but only a few recipes, a very few. These recipes and the subsequent joys they will bring to you come from the small community of Guardia Lombardy, a hilltop paradise some 3,000 feet above sea level, protected from the ever-growing populations of the larger urban areas of Salerno, Naples and Avellino. There is no reason for an outsider to visit Guardia Lombardy, unless he has family there. And there is no reason for one to leave Guardia Lombardy today unless, of course, he tires of pure mountain air, panoramic views of olive orchards, acres of fruit and nut trees and Italian cooking that not even Alfredo of Rome would be so bold to imitate.

So, then, permit me to show you how easy it is to prepare simple, tasteful meals for an intimate occasion, or for friends and family, whose exposure to Italian cooking has been pizza, lasagna or spaghetti American style at the local Grizzly Bear.

There are few places where you will be able to taste and enjoy such creations as pasta e fagioli, or lenticchia e pasta. It is doubtful if you will find a place to buy these delights of Guardia Lombardy; or I know of no one in this magnificent and beautiful and gorgeously created land who has the secrets of these special peasant foods.

And along with these secrets will be revealed the more intimate details of when to serve, how to serve and to whom to serve these Italian peasant foods. Your family, your friends or your whomever will be beholden to you for these recipes, which will surely be the food of the future for they contain the real life ingredients.

the foods

I can remember when pasta was the essential source of nutrition for an Italian. Pasta was to an Italian what rice was or still is to an Oriental. This dependency meant only one thing . . . the pasta had to be of the highest quality.

I can still hear my mother's voice when instructing us while shopping: "Always look for the best."

Her favorite line was and probably still is, "You don't put junk in your stomach; you put it in the garbage pail."

Italian peasant food can be wholesome as well as interesting.

In those days we had an ice box where a 2 x 2 foot square piece of ice, costing 30 cents, was placed in the upper chamber and covered with old newspapers. It kept our food fresh until used. We always had fresh items in the ice box. It was never stocked with jars of relishes or other supplemental foods.

My dear Italian mother bought fresh foods every day. She seldom had packaged pasta for very long, either. She never bought bulk pasta, always packaged, insisting that if it was opened or bulk it would lose some of its vitality. Whether it did or not is debatable. But I never argued with her about food. Even today, whenever I visit my mother and look into the refrigerator it contains only fresh foods. She buys only what she needs for the day with the exception of milk or juice.

"I cook, and you be the student," she would say whenever in later years I tried to offer a suggestion regarding modern concepts of food.

Her advice has gone a long way. In selecting pasta, I recommend to buy the best because pasta is the least expensive ingredient of your meal, but the most essential.

Good Italian pasta is available in most of the large supermarkets. Buy pasta made from hard red winter wheat or durum wheat No. 1 semolina. Pasta made from soft wheat is for chinese noodles and pastry. Check the package carefully. Don't buy it unless you are satisfied with the contents.

In another page, I have illustrated all types of macaroni available. They are macaroni manufactured by the Ronzoni Macaroni Company, Inc., of Long Island, a company dating back to my childhood.

Other companies have products that are as good but I'm not familiar with them. I know that Ronzoni today is distributed nation-wide.

Many non-Italians refer to pasta as spaghetti whether the macaroni is linguine, spaghettini (thin spaghetti), perciatelli or any other style.

Spaghetti is only one style of pasta designed to go with certain meals. For instance, if you are making lasagna you never use spaghetti or any of the thin style macaroni. Lasagna calls for large size noodles, measuring about one inch in width. The reason is simple: You need large sized noodles to hold the ingredients. As you can see in the illustrations on pages 16-19, macaroni comes in many shapes and sizes to accommodate the taste or whim of the cook.

Pasta, however, is only one type of peasant cooking. I plan to call attention to other frequently used items in my Italian peasant cooking so that you can enjoy these good foods as I do.

Let's talk about olive oil. Now, this is quite important. I would recommend buying 100 per cent olive oil. Never substitute half olive oil and salad oil for a recipe which calls for olive oil. The only time you can depart from this suggestion, and I would not suggest doing it too often, is using part olive oil and part salad oil for salads. Olive oil is expensive and always has been. However, it is necessary. Another thing to remember is to buy only Italian style olive oil; not Greek, Spanish or other types. Italian olive oil has a certain consistency which works with the foods mentioned here. The olive oil can be either domestic or imported.

Tomato sauce. Ah! There's the secret to much of the success of these recipes. Never have I tasted Italian tomato sauce that compares with my mother's. She prepares her sauce with Italian style plum tomatoes. Some of the brand names are Contadina, Progresso or any other Italian brand. Again, either an import or domestic. My mother prefers Progresso.

Many years ago she would buy boxes of plum style tomatoes and make her own sauce. This process would take several days. I would remember the kitchen activity during those days. Huge pots of boiling tomatoes for hours and hours. One day it was cooking the sauce; the next it was pouring the sauce into mason jars and stacking them into the kitchen pantry.

Back in the 30's, the Italians in Newark made practically all their food at home, including macaroni.

However, as the years passed, small companies catering to Italian-Americans, began to develop, supplying the culinary needs of this population.

One item of food that deserves notice here and which is overlooked most of the time, is grated cheese. Parmesan cheese should be of the highest quality for grating. The Roma brand was a popular label during my youth. It may still be today. Nevertheless, look for a store that sells bulk cheese for grating. Generally this cheese is very dry and old and too sharp to eat straight. Sprinkle some on your pasta and it gives another dimension to the taste. Grated cheese is also good in soups and on salads.

Another favored item is Italian bread. We always ate Italian bread sans butter and unheated. Italian bread has a thick crust, much thicker than that found on sourdough French. Generally, we bought bread directly from the bakery. Every neighborhood had a bakery which served maybe a two or three block radius of population. The Italian bread contains flour, yeast, salt and water.

We never buttered our bread during lunch or dinner. Butter was never on the table. It was used only on toast in the morning. The butter was a high quality sweet butter which my father applied liberally on his one slice of toast daily.

Everyone knows Italians drink wine with their meals. Never after meals, unless, of course, you have extended conversation. I remember during the holidays my mother would place some large Freestone peaches on the table and a bowl of mixed nuts. The peaches were sliced and dipped into the wine and eaten with a fork or fingers. We would intersperse this with a variety of nuts, from almonds to filberts to walnuts. Italians love filberts and almonds. However, if the meal was to end without this post social dinner gathering we would leave the table and do whatever we were supposed to do . . . empty the garbage, homework, or if it were summer, go out and play kick-the-can until dark. My parents would retire to the living room and talk about the day's activities without wine or coffee. My father never wanted anything after his dinner. "It would spoil my digestion," he would say. He still continues this routine at age 78.

Back to my wine. The wine we served was generally a light burgundy or if the meal was a highly spiced Italian stew, then we had the hearty barbarone. However, it was usually Burgundy, Zinfandel or Chianti. Usually a good red table wine in the low to medium price range compares with the wine we consumed during our meals.

The wine was dry; not sweet. It was light and several glasses would bring on an avalanche of interrupting conversation and laughter. There were always two or three or more conversations in progress during the weekend meal or holiday meals with adult guests. As children, we never talked at the table unless we were spoken to first.

Remembering these scenes is reliving moments of true family love, something that held me together and has given me strength during my adult years.

15

pastas

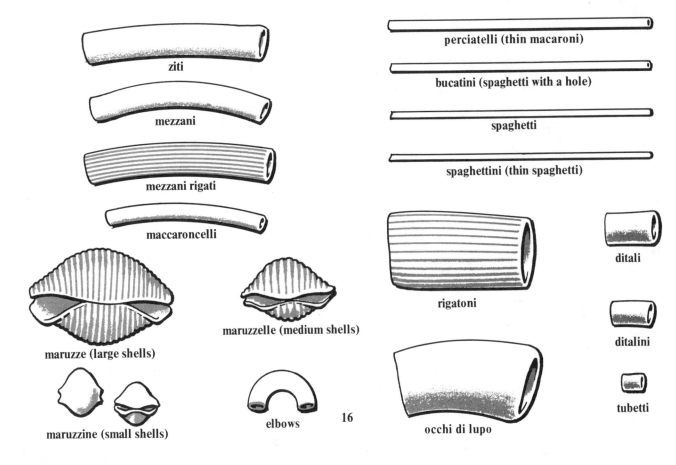

ziti

mezzani

mezzani rigati

maccaroncelli

perciatelli (thin macaroni)

bucatini (spaghetti with a hole)

spaghetti

spaghettini (thin spaghetti)

rigatoni

ditali

ditalini

tubetti

maruzze (large shells)

maruzzelle (medium shells)

maruzzine (small shells)

elbows

16

occhi di lupo

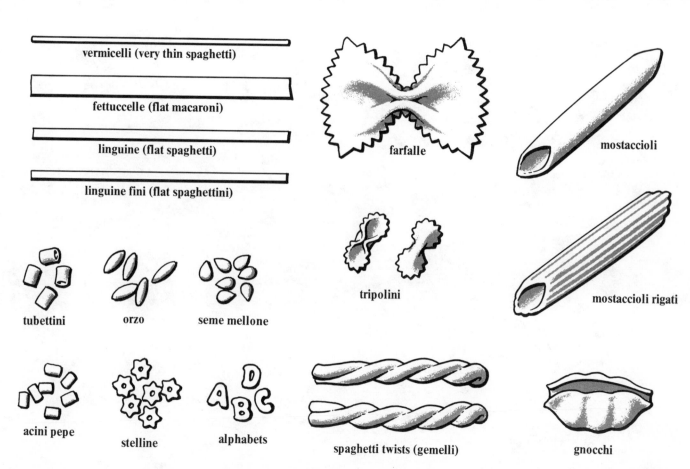

vermicelli (very thin spaghetti)

fettuccelle (flat macaroni)

linguine (flat spaghetti)

linguine fini (flat spaghettini)

farfalle

mostaccioli

tripolini

mostaccioli rigati

tubettini

orzo

seme mellone

acini pepe

stelline

alphabets

spaghetti twists (gemelli)

gnocchi

17

pastas

creste di gallo

tortellini

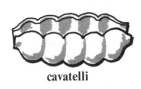

cavatelli

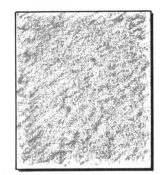

lasagne (extra wide)

mafalde

margherite

rotelle

riccini

fusilli bucati

18

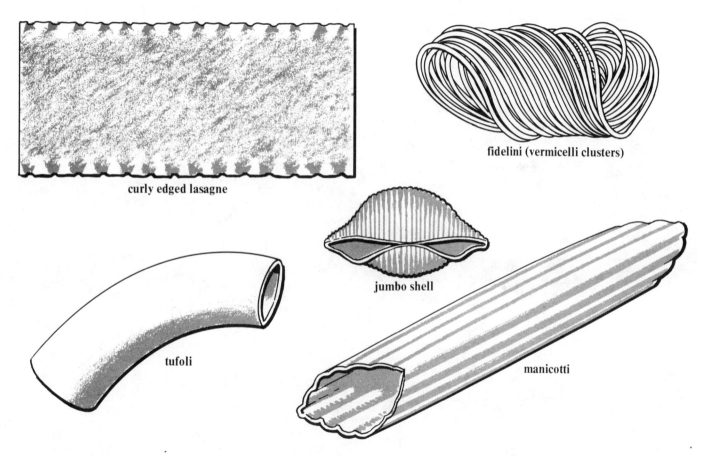

curly edged lasagne

fidelini (vermicelli clusters)

jumbo shell

tufoli

manicotti

19

ragu e braciola
tomato sauce with meat

During most of my youth I heard, "Today I have to make my gravy". When I left the environs of my native Newark I began hearing the word "gravy" bantered about, only to find out it meant flour and water flavored with meat, not tomato sauce. We never called it anything but gravy or ragu; seldom, tomato sauce.

Here is the simple yet satisfying way to make tomato meat sauce or ragu or "gravy," Neapolitan style:

Place olive oil, 1 onion, and a little lard in a frying pan, When you feel the flavor of the lard and onion have been transferred to the oil, remove them. Then brown two pork chops in the oil and when that is done set it aside.

Now, we prepare the rolled round steak, which has been cut thin (about 1/4"). The round steak should be a little over a pound. This is called braciola. Place the round steak on the table where you are cooking, spread it out. Place some raisins, parsley, thin strips of provalone cheese, garlic and grated romano cheese on the steak. Add black pepper, roll and tie with white string. Brown in frying pan.

The meat balls are next: Combine 1 lb (total) of ground beef, veal and pork, add 3/4 cup of bread crumbs (my mother made her own), two tablespoons of grated cheese, raisins, garlic, parsley, black pepper and two eggs. Form into balls and brown on all sides. Add the meatballs, the rolled beef and the pork chops to two cans of tomatoes (2 lb size) and one can of tomato paste. Add salt, pepper and fresh basil to taste and cook slowly for 1-1/2 to 2 hours. Excellent to pour over ravioli and other pasta.

salsicce italiane

italian sausage, broiled of course

One of the current favorites in this affluent period is Italian sausage. I remember the days when sausage was king and we could merely afford the aroma only and left the rest to imagination. Thank God for that wonderful Italian imagination. Without that, what a desert we would live in.

Back to Italian sausage. First you must find a market which sells sausage of this kind. The sausages are about four times the size of the ordinary link sausage you see in the market, roughly the size of thick frankfurters.

Get two pounds of sausage, two green peppers, and of course, olive oil and you're on your way. Slice the green pepper in 1/2" width and saute in the olive oil. Set the peppers aside. Broil the sausage for about 30 minutes or until well done and brown on all sides. Before serving, pour green peppers over the top. This should serve three or four. Serve with Italian or French bread and some strong dry red wine. I prefer a hearty burgundy.

costolette di polo
chicken cutlets

Chicken was a delicacy in those impoverished years of the 30's. A chicken roasted or fricasseed and seasoned with spicy tomato sauce was a treat to behold. But whenever my dear Italian mother decided to prepare chicken cutlets we drooled and paid proper homage to her culinary wisdom. This dish was served only on special occasions.

Begin by using one pound of chicken breast cutlets. But breasts only, and remove the bone and slice as thin as you possibly can. Wash, drain and thoroughly dry chicken with paper towels. My mother always used a dish towel, since we didn't have paper towels. Dip into a specially prepared coating mixture and then add egg mixture. Fry slowly in large skillet, using corn oil. Then drain on towel. It should serve 3.

> 1 lb breast of cutlets
> 1 cup of coating mixture which consists of 2/3 cup of cracker meal
>   and 1/3 cup of flour
> Egg mixture consists of two eggs, parsley, salt to taste, pepper
>   and grated cheese
> Mix and beat well.

veal piazziola e spaghetti
veal cutlets with spaghetti

To most diners of Italian food, meatballs are as much part of a delicious spaghetti meal as fragrant Chianti wine is part of Italian life.

However, few realize that there is another meat dish which adds supreme taste to spaghetti – and that is veal piazziola – truly a dish for the gods.

The sauce from veal piazziola is poured over the cooked spaghetti and served as the only sauce. Few, if any, Italian restaurants serve this combination.

Your veal must be prepared almost paper thin. Use about 6-8 veal cutlets the size of your hand. Pounding the cutlets between two sheets of wax paper is an excellent method of thinning to your preference.

This is what you will need:

  6-8 veal cutlets
  1 cup canned tomatoes
  2 tbsp olive oil
  Salt, pepper, oregano and one clove of garlic chopped very fine

Place the cutlets in a shallow baking pan, preferably pyrex. Others will do. Cover with oil, tomatoes, and add spices to taste. Bake at 350° for about one hour. Remove the cutlets and use the sauce to pour over a side dish of spaghetti. This is often served with green peas and serves 4. A light red wine and bread and you need not worry about the ills of life.

costolette di vitello
veal cutlets

Veal cutlets were always a special meal. The thing I remember most about cutlets was that on the day after they were served we would always have cold cutlets in sandwiches.

Nothing is as good for the soul as a veal cutlet sandwich. The cutlet is served cold but has been breaded and fried.

My mother never bought prepared mixture for breading. She always made her own.

This is what you will need:
    6 paper thin veal cutlets
    3 eggs
    1 cup flour
    Salt, pepper, chopped fresh Italian parsley and 1/2 cup of olive oil

Mix the flour, salt and pepper. Then in a separate dish beat the eggs and add salt, pepper and parsley. Dip the cutlets first in the flour mixture and then into the egg mixture.

Fry in a large frying pan, using olive oil. Cook slowly, turning cutlets when browned and then drain on a paper towel. Serves 3 or 4.

calamaio

squid

To a child the idea of stuffed squid is not in the least appealing. However, it is a meal which reminds me of holidays or festive occasions. Whenever squid or as my mother called it "Calamaio" was mentioned it meant a treat. Not for me, but for my Dad, who now that I think of it, was treated like a king. My brother always said "he's got it made. The food is waiting for him when he gets up. It's there when he comes home for lunch and for dinner. He doesn't do any handy man chores, walks around in his suit and lives the life of a real gentleman." I have to agree. I never saw my Dad without his shirt in the summer and always with his jacket and vest during the winter and autumn months. Once I remember he departed from his role as King of the Household. For some unexplained reason he decided to paint the wrought iron railing. I don't know why he did this. But he got himself some paint and started the job. My father was a highly disciplined person whenever he did anything.

When I came home and saw him painting, my second reaction after the initial one of seeing him at a handy man chore was what in the heck was he doing painting the railing while still wearing his suit and hat.

"Dad, why don't you change into some old clothes?" I asked.

"Why? I don't intend to paint my clothes, merely the railing."

And now you know why my dear Italian mother treated this man with the utmost respect. I learned later that the reason he painted the railing was to satisfy a whim of my mother who decided no one else could do the job.

That was the only time I saw him actually do manual work. I did the gardening, always helping my mother who enjoyed the outdoor activity. But sometimes I wonder whether she actually did or whether someone suggested it would be a healthy activity and a relief from the heat of the kitchen.

Anyhow, back to the squid, my father's favorite.

Here's the recipe:
> 4 squid
> 2 cups Italian bread crumbs, made at home
> 3 tbsp olive oil, parsley, oregano, black pepper, finely cut garlic
>   and raisins to taste
> 3 cups of tomatoes

Thoroughly clean the squid and remove inside bone and outer skin. Wash in salted water and drain while preparing stuffing.

Mix bread crumbs with olive oil, spices, garlic and raisins until crumbs are wet. Stuff squid and sew close with white thread. Fry in olive oil, browning slowly and turning often. Place in saucepan and drain frying oil into saucepan. Add tomatoes, fresh parsley and salt. Cook until tender. Do not overcook as squid tends to toughen. Serves 4-6.

brodo di polo
chicken soup

I've heard the word "love" used so often that it sounds like someone telling me to have "a good day". Does that person really want me to have a good day? Maybe so. Maybe it's merely habit. Saying "have a good day" is like saying "I love you". Remember the flower children of the 60's who passed out flowers and "loved" everyone. Maybe that was love. Or the mother who constantly reminds her neglected child "I love you". Maybe it's habit. But still to me the words "I love you" sound empty. I know you must say something but sometimes saying isn't actually feeling.

During my youth I never once heard "I love you". But I knew when my mother had my clothes ready for me for school, when she bundled me against the frigid Newark cold or when she had a warm meal which she put together from the meager earnings of a Depression tailor, there was one hell of a lot of love there. There was no obligation. No hangups. And who then ever heard of Dr. Spock? She cared and that was love. I knew there would be lunch for me and then dinner which *she* prepared; not Ms. Campbell. Or the nights she held me in her arms against her chest trying to ease the pain of an agonizing earache. That's love. I felt the warmth of her body surging through me, telling me it would all be fine. To me that's love and to this day, though my mother may still find it difficult to say it I know love is there.

So what brings me to this is the meal that has made mothers famous all over the eastern United States – chicken soup.

It's not that chicken soup is all that great. But what makes chicken soups the savior for an ailing body is the person who prepared it. In all cases it's the mother. And my dear Italian mother was no exception. When you are ailing, the best chicken and the finest broth could not in any way surpass the love that is transmitted from the person who makes the soup for you. I guess it is the caring that goes into the soup that makes the broth.

These are the practical ingredients for Momma's chicken soup. Choose a 4 to 5 pound ready-to-cook chicken and cut into pieces. Legs, wings, breasts, etc. Place the cut up chicken in a pot and add water just to cover the chicken pieces. To this add a half teaspoon of salt per pound of chicken. Add some fresh parsley, a stalk of celery, a carrot, a leek, and one fresh tomato. Bring all this to a boil and then reduce the heat. Skim the fat from time to time. Cover the pot containing the chicken and vegetables and simmer for about three hours or until the chicken is tender. Remove the chicken from broth. Cut up small pieces of the chicken and the carrot to use in escarole soup (see page 47). Use remaining chicken to eat (salad or with fried green peppers). (See page 67.)

marinara salsa

tomato sauce

1 2-lb can of tomatoes
1/4 cup olive oil
1 clove garlic
1 tsp salt
Oregano and parsley to taste

Saute garlic in oil. Remove garlic and add tomatoes (strained) and spices. Cook slowly for about 45 minutes. Best on spaghetti and light pasta.

linguine or spaghetti con aglio e olio di oliva

linguine or spaghetti with garlic and olive oil

There comes a time when you just don't know what to prepare for that very special friend who enjoys an excitement beyond the unknown. I have entertained many knowledgeable cooks who have been more than suitably impressed with the following dish. It is a hurry-up delight which satisfies, entertains and absolutely mystifies your guest. It is a dish which deserves an audience. It requires the epitome of flamboyancy. Never, absolutely never, deprive your guest of seeing you create linguine or spaghetti con aglio e olio, or simply said, spaghetti with garlic and oil. The difference between linguine and spaghetti is linguine is a flattened spaghetti.

This pasta dish is more theater than anything else. In fact, most Italian food is kitchen theater. My mother! Did she perform for us. I remember once bringing some friends over from New York for a hurry-up meal because we were on our way back to school.

We gathered around the kitchen and watched her prepare with gusto, spaghetti with oil and garlic.

She opened a package of Ronzoni Italian spaghetti No. 8, a one-pound package and placed that on the table. Then she filled a pan with four quarts of water and heated it. She poured a few drops of oil in the water and a pinch of salt. The oil was to prevent the macaroni from sticking together. When the water came to a boil, she put in the spaghetti and was careful not to break the spaghetti. As the spaghetti boiled, she prepared the other ingredients.

She peeled about four cloves of garlic and opened a can of anchovies. (The latter is optional but for real taste, she used anchovies.) She then poured about 3 ounces of olive oil in a deep frying pan. She also placed her oregano, salt and pepper within easy reach and then waited for the spaghetti to be ready.

As the pasta approached completion, which takes 10 to 12 minutes, she began heating the oil in which she had placed the garlic cloves. As the cloves turned light brown over a slow-medium heat she put in the anchovies. By this time the pasta was ready. She drained the water and let the spaghetti sit in the colander for a few minutes.

When the oil was just hot enough but not smoking, in went the spaghetti. She stirred the mixture vigorously so that the oil, garlic and all other ingredients got used to each other. A friend of mine in latter years when he witnessed my performance re-marked he had never seen spaghetti sauteed!

You can also add other delights to this mixture depending on your whim. Sometimes I toss in a few cut up mushrooms and some slivered almonds. This dish can be prepared simply or lavishly depending on the occasion. Keep in mind this is a poverty dish so to keep it authentic use only garlic, oil and spaghetti with some salt and pepper.

Here's the recipe for four:

1 lb spaghetti or linguine	1/2 tsp salt
3 ounces olive oil	1/2 tsp pepper
4 cloves fresh garlic	small can anchovies (optional)

ravioli
ravioli

No Italian restaurant on the West Coast or even the East could possibly duplicate my mother's ravioli. They not only taste different, but look different, and the restaurant ravioli pale in comparison.

First of all, the restaurant ravioli I've encountered, and there may be exceptions, are small – measuring 2x2 and contain spinach or meat – seldom, if ever, ricotta (Italian cottage cheese).

My mother's ravioli are larger and can give the cook unlimited pleasure.

If it was a holiday and we were good we could expect ravioli. But we were never sure. Oh! The power of the kitchen. My mother wielded that power with the finesse of Iturbi playing Mozart. Magnificent was her ravioli. Omnipotent was her power. To us my mother was all things. Absolutely no joy compares to a Neapolitan ravioli aptly seasoned with ragu.

Throughout the years ravioli was the feasts of feasts. It was the epitome of the holiday. When we ate ravioli it was a celebration.

In my youth, the holidays, particularly Easter, meant ravioli, meats, fine wine, conversation and pasta dolce.

Above all, ravioli was king.

To prepare ravioli you must first get Italian ricotta. It is a cheese made from goat's milk. The ricotta is prepared first. Take one pound of ricotta, some raisins, a little parsley, sprinkle of cinnamon, some black pepper, grated cheese and two eggs. Mix well and place in bowl and chill until you have made the ravioli dough.

What is needed for ravioli dough is two cups of white unbleached flour, one egg and lukewarm water.

Place flour on large board. Make a well in center and drop in the egg. Add water a little at a time, enough to make a smooth feeling dough. Knead on a floured board.

Place in a covered bowl and allow to rest for 10 minutes. Then roll dough out on board one half at a time, cut into long strips about 3-4 inches wide. Drop one table-spoon of ricotta filling at 2-inch intervals. Cover with another strip, cut with a dough cutter and pinch edges with a fork to seal. Place the individual ravioli on the floured board while meat sauce cooks or until ravioli pasta is dry.

When ravioli is dry (about 1/2 hour) place in boiling water and cook for 10 minutes or until tender. Pour in colander and then place in large serving plate and pour ragu over it.

Recipe for filling:

1 lb ricotta	black pepper
raisins	grated cheese
parsley	2 eggs
cinnamon	

35

cavitelli con broccoli
pasta with broccoli

Broccoli is a vegetable which most people feel must be cooked alone or with more broccoli or maybe with a small onion or two. But never with anything but another vegetable.

However, this recipe which calls for pasta with broccoli is more exciting than my spaghetti with garlic and oil (see page 32).

It was a perfect Friday night dish which we occasionally substituted for fish.

First, brown some garlic in olive oil. Remove the garlic and then add salt and red crushed pepper.

Cook broccoli and pasta in two separate saucepans until tender. When they are cooked add to the olive oil and simmer together slowly until all flavors are combined. Serves 4.

The cavitelli are tube pasta about two inches long and 1/8 or 1/4 inch in diameter. If you can't locate this type of pasta at your store, try any other pasta which has a hole but larger than 1/4 inch in diameter. You will sometimes find long macaroni with holes which can be broken into pieces of about 2-3 inches. Perciatelli is one. Small rigatoni can be used.

1/2 lb cavitelli
1/2 lb broccoli
6 tbsp olive oil
1 clove of garlic
1/2 tsp salt
Red crushed pepper to taste

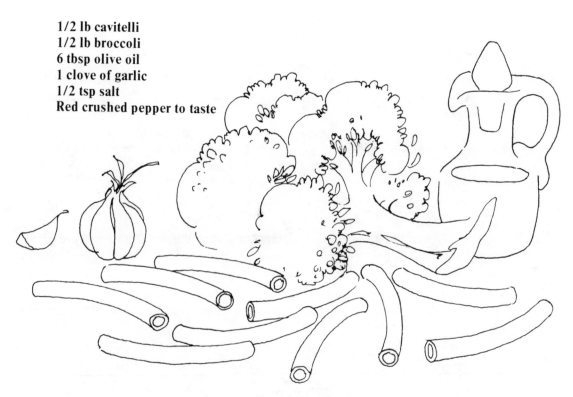

pasta e piselli
shell macaroni and peas

This is a dish which I know you can never get in any restaurant that serves Italian food. It is simple but extremely tasty and easy to prepare for a noon snack or as an introduction to meat entree.

I recommend small shell macaroni because they can mingle closely with the peas. The more aggressive shells may even go so far as to embrace the peas and you get miniature macaroni-pea sandwich. I'm getting ahead of my story here. Let's back up and get the ingredients out on the table before we begin. First, get your shell macaroni (hard winter wheat), one 8-1/2 oz. can of sweet peas, olive oil, can of tomatoes, parsley, garlic, basil and black pepper. Now, we begin.

Cook all the ingredients (except the pasta and peas) slowly in a saucepan. Usually about 1/2 hour.

Cook the pasta in a separate pan until tender. Before straining, add strained peas and then strain both immediately. Pour pasta and peas into tomato sauce (see recipe for marinara sauce, page 31) and simmer just a few minutes so that all the flavors are absorbed. Serve hot. Serves 4.

3/4 lb shell macaroni
1-8-1/2 oz can sweet peas
2 cups of Italian peeled tomatoes
sprig of parsley
1 clove of garlic
a few leaves of basil
1/4 tsp black pepper

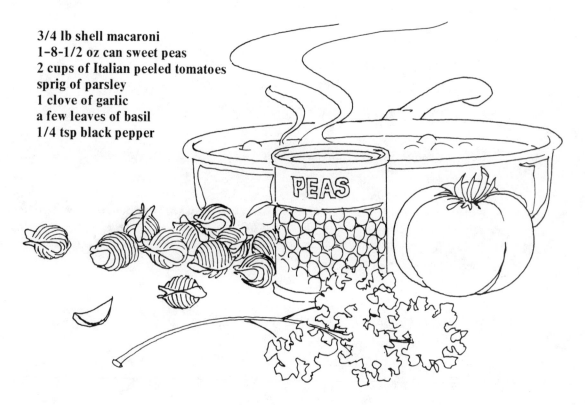

pasta e potata

macaroni and potatoes

It was a three block walk from 15th Avenue Grammar School to home. During those cold Newark winters it was a long three blocks, particularly when you had to come home for lunch and then go back to school.

Many times our lunch for those cold wintry days was macaroni and potatoes. There were no school lunches in those days. No one took a lunch because there was no cafeteria.

My mother would cut up or dice the potatoes in 1/2" squares and then place them in boiling water for 3 minutes. She then added ditalini No. 40 or tubettini (which means small tube). See the chart on page 16. She would boil the macaroni until tender. She would then drain all but 1/4 cup of the boiled water and pour in 1/4 cup of marinara sauce (see page 31). The macaroni and potatoes would be cooked together for a few minutes and the mixture was served steaming hot.

pasta e fagioli
macaroni and beans

One dish reminds me of my youth in the Depression more than any others. It's pasta e fagioli or more specifically, short (2 inches) pieces of macaroni and white beans. This was the ultimate in peasant food. When you were served pasta e fagioli, it meant nothing else was to follow. It was the meal served before payday. With pasta e fagioli you had the anti-pasta entree in one serving. Occasionally, a simple lettuce salad was served with it, and of course, Italian bread.

Here's the recipe:

> 1/2 lb ditalini (pasta dried in tubular form about 1/4 inch in diameter and 1/4 inch long)
> 1 cup of Italian plum style tomatoes
> 1/2 cup of canned cannelini beans
> 1 tbsp olive oil

First, cook the ditalini. When they are ready, prepare the sauce. Cook clove of garlic in olive oil and add tomatoes. Remove the garlic. Add oregano, salt and pepper. Then add the cooked pasta (ditalini) and beans to sauce and allow to simmer together for 5 minutes. Serves 4.

If you are unable to find the canned cannelini beans, use plain white dried beans. They must be soaked overnight and then cooked for about 30 minutes or until tender. Use slightly less than 1/2 cup of the dried beans with this recipe.

42

potata e sedano

potatoes and celery

If anyone should tell you today that celery and spuds make an interesting meal, you might consider yourself in the presence of a fool. But, as I was preparing this book, my sister reminded me that my dear Italian mother did actually prepare that combination. I don't remember it as potata e sedano. I do remember, "Tonight, we have aach." The accent is on the double "a". Then, I remembered that delicious combination which gave us strength and good tummies.

My mother parboiled the potatoes. When that was done, she set them aside to begin the next ritual. She browned garlic in olive oil and then removed the garlic. Some prefer keeping the garlic with the food, but that is so gauche. Remove it and then add 1 cup canned tomatoes, some salt, fresh parsley and celery leaves. Cook slowly and as tomatoes boil add 1/2 cup of water. Cook the sauce for 15 minutes. Then add potatoes and cook together with celery leaves until tender.

Here are the ingredients:
    4 potatoes diced into small pieces
    1/2 head of celery leaves
    1 cup canned tomatoes
    1/2 tsp. salt
    Parsley, one clove garlic and 2 tbsp olive oil

escarole con olio
escarole with oil

Another favorite dish of mine was escarole with oil. It was also one of my father's favorites.

This was served on a week night. My father would always arrive home about 5:30 p.m., and when he walked in, he sniffed the air then broke into that beautiful smile of his and complimented my mother:

"I smelled that all the way down the block." He gave my mother a big grin and then hurried upstairs to wash. By the time he was downstairs, the meal was ready to be served. My father would have had no time for a "pick-me-upper" if he was so inclined. And if he were my mother certainly would have admonished him with "You want to spoil your appetite?" She has said that to me, a member of the "drink before dinner" set, whenever I visited in later years.

We seldom, if ever, drank anything before meals during my youth. During meals it was something else. My father would have a glass of wine and in the summer, a glass or two of beer. We never overindulged.

My mother made a variety of vegetables but it was a special treat when she made escarole. It is easy to prepare and one of the more delicious uses of the greens.

Cut the escarole in small pieces, discarding the tough outer leaves. Soak in salted water for about five minutes, drain and wash thoroughly. My mother always soaked vegetables in salted water because it produced a more efficient cleansing effect.

After the escarole is washed and drained, begin to prepare the oil. Heat oil, garlic, parsley, celery, salt, water and pepper in saucepan for 10 minutes. Remove garlic and then add escarole, cooking slowly for about 20-30 minutes. Serves 4-6.

Ingredients are:
   2 lbs escarole
   1 clove of garlic
   4 tbsp olive oil
   1/2 cup of water
   green parsley
   leafy piece of celery
   salt and pepper to taste

46

escarole con salsa di pomodoro
escarole in tomato sauce

My mother also prepared escarole in tomato sauce (see page 31). Before you place the escarole in the sauce wash it thoroughly and cook until almost tender, then place in the mixture. Several medium heads of escarole will serve four to five. For string beans, Italian style, substitute string beans for the escarole.

brodo di polo con escarole
escarole in chicken broth

Clean and boil escarole for a few minutes. Place in saucepan of chicken broth adding grated cheese to escarole. (See Momma's Chicken Soup, page 28.)

asparagi con formaggio
asparagus with cheese

And then there were the days when Milton Cross commanded the attention of every Italian opera lover on the East Coast on Saturday. Did I detest listening to Galli Gurci, Martinelli and the others who lured my Dad close to his radio. I remember Dad in the dining room listening to the Crosley – sitting about two feet from it, and Mom in the kitchen preparing the Saturday night special.

It was an afternoon of screeching and deep baritones. I was in the grade school at the time, and what I wanted to listen to was something with a little more zap. I got my way when the Hit Parade came on later that evening.

Whenever I listen to the classics today, more specifically my favorite Italian operas, I occasionally think of Milton Cross, the radio commentator who was the voice of Texaco introducing the Metropolitan Opera for the Saturday radio fans. He was as familiar to me as Martin Block of the Make Believe Ballroom. Block occupied top billing on WNEW for years.

Saturday night was vegetables and meat. Sometimes lamb chops, a scalopini, or whatever Dad was in the mood for.

However, Mom would never go totally American on us. One dish I remember was asparagi parmigiana (asparagus with parmesan).

All you need for this dish is one bunch of fresh asparagus, olive oil and parmesan cheese. Wash the asparagus. Cut off the tough ends and remove the scales. Scrub and cook in rapidly boiling salted water until partially tender. Drain and place in a baking dish. Add olive oil and sprinkle generously with grated parmesan cheese. Bake in a hot oven for about 10 minutes or until cheese browns. Serves 4.

    1 bunch fresh asparagus
    2 tbsp olive oil
    Grated parmesan cheese
    Salt to taste

cici e tagliatelli
chick peas and noodles

I like plenty of good Italian or French bread within reach when I prepare Cici e Tagliatelli or chick peas and noodles.

As in all my mother's favorite pasta dishes only hard winter wheat macaroni was used. The reason for this is that macaroni made from hard red winter wheat will hold up better while cooking.

To begin this simple but tasty dish you will need two cups of Italian peeled tomatoes, parsley, garlic, some basil, chick peas, black ground pepper and 3/16 of an inch flat noodles.

Cook all ingredients slowly in a saucepan (except chick peas and noodles). Usually for 1/2 hour. Cook noodles in boiling salted water to desired tenderness. Before completely cooked, add chick peas and cook together for a few minutes. Strain and pour into saucepan of sauce. Mama, mia! I can practically taste it now. Cook slowly in sauce until some liquid is absorbed. It should not be too soupy. Serve this immediately. Serves 4-5.

1/2 can of chick peas (strained)
3/4 lb of 3/16 inch flat noodles
3 tablespoons of olive oil
2 cups of Italian peeled tomatoes
sprig of parsley
1 clove of garlic
a few leaves of basil
1/4 tsp of black pepper

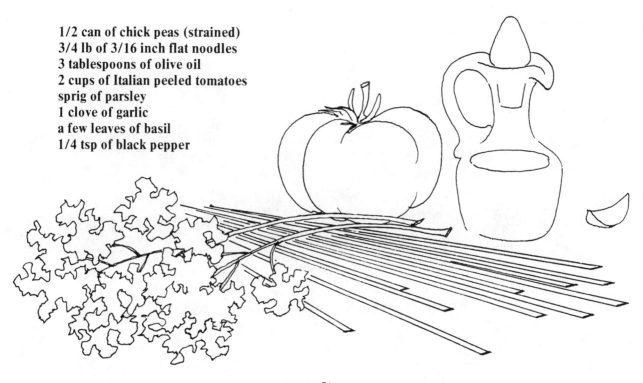

piselli con uova
peas with eggs

Whenever I think of piselli con uova (peas with eggs) I remember 15th Street, the Maple tree-lined street which was my territory between South Orange Avenue to the north and 14th Avenue to the south – one block of childhood memories.

I remember piselli con uova being served on a Wednesday night. Each day had certain foods and they seldom changed from week to week. It was ritual. The only exception would be on holidays. For instance, Thursday night was always spaghetti, and Tuesday another pasta dish. Friday, of course, was fish night. Wednesday was piselli con uova.

For some reason I always think of 15th Street with piselli con uova. Maybe it's because in our up-and-down duplex whenever we served this dish it was an occasion for our neighbors, the Cohns, to visit with their native food in hand and exchange for piselli con uova. I remember Gladys, a daughter of the Cohns, a buxom blond whom I ogled, would come inviting an exchange of native dishes. We were always happy to give her a hot plate of the peas with eggs and then we reluctantly accepted her offering. To this day I can't remember what it was because we never ate it. I think my mother placed it in the ice box and heated it for one of the delivery men who always seemed to be hungry whenever they came to our door.

To prepare peas with eggs you first heat oil in a large saucepan, add some onion and cook until the onion is translucent. Then add tomatoes and simmer for 15-20 minutes. Add the peas, some salt and pepper and cook for about 10 more minutes. Drop each beaten egg into the sauce one at a time, gently. Cook slowly. Eggs should take about 4 minutes. Serves 4.

  4 eggs (beaten)
  2 tbsp olive oil
  1 chopped onion
  2 cups of Italian peeled tomatoes
  1 large can of peas
  salt and pepper to taste

lenticchie e sedano
lentils and celery

Those cold winter days in Newark were unbearable. Ear muffs, mittens, pea jackets, wool caps were the essentials. The ponds in the parks were always frozen, much to the happiness of the ice skaters. That was the only winter sport in which we could indulge. Newark had no mountains, no rushing streams, only the ponds and the putrid Passaic River. So we put our energies into ice skating. And, if it snowed, we went sledding. After a day's hard outdoor activity we looked forward to a warm nourishing meal. Invariably, Mom prepared lentils and celery.

The dish has an excellent protein content. I like using Italian or French breads with this meal and a glass of good red table wine. A small green salad, some cheese and you have a good light, sufficient meal.

Mom would soak the lentils for an hour in lukewarm water. She would then heat the water with the lentils to a boiling point and then drain the lentils. After that was done she would add freshly boiled water to the lentils and salt and allow to boil slowly on a very low flame or heat for 1-1/2 hours.

She would then boil mixture of oil, garlic, tomatoes and parsley for 10 minutes. Then the lentils were added plus the celery, which had been boiled in a separate pan earlier. Be sure to use dark green cooking celery. Cook for about 15 minutes. Serves 4.

1/2 box lentils or one cup
1 celery stalk (chopped)
1/2 cup olive oil
1 clove garlic
1-1/4 cup tomatoes
chopped parsley
salt to taste

lenticchie e pasta
lentils and pasta

Follow recipe for lentils and celery. Substitute tiny cooked shell pasta for celery. Cook pasta and lentils together for only a few minutes to absorb all flavors.

carciofi imbottiti
stuffed artichokes

When I moved to Portland in the mid-50's I found artichokes a rare item in that city's supermarkets. Artichokes were virtually unknown to the Portland home. As the years went by and other cuisines became avant garde, artichokes began appearing. However their preparation was simple and unimaginative when compared to the delicacy prepared for our dinner table by my mother. Boiling artichokes and then dipping the leaves in melted butter or mayonnaise was unheard of.

Artichokes are a Mediterranean delight, an extra touch to an Italian meal. My mother served artichokes stuffed with bread crumbs, anchovy filets and dressed with olive oil.

The first thing is to cut off stems and remove the tough outer leaves. Wash the artichokes and shake thoroughly to rid of water.

Mix bread crumbs, anchovies, garlic, parsley, cheese, salt and pepper. Stuff the mixture between leaves of each artichoke. Close and place in saucepan so artichokes are standing close to each other to support the leaves and stuffing. Also, it is a good idea to wrap string around each artichoke. When that is done pour olive oil over each artichoke. and a small amount of water to cause some vapor. Cover the pan and cook until tender, usually about 30-45 minutes.

Here are the ingredients:

    4 large artichokes
    1-1/2 cups home-made bread crumbs (my mother never bought the store kind)
    4 anchovy filets
    3 tbsp chopped Italian parsley, grated cheese, salt and pepper to taste

The bread crumbs are made from either stale Italian or French bread.

peperoni imbottiti
stuffed peppers

There is nothing more satisfying when you are in a temper tantrum than to toss a peperoni imbottiti across the room and watch it splatter into a door with glorious instant color. I've done it. The windup and delivery were superb; only the outcome was disastrous.

Whenever I see a peperoni imbottiti, I remember that awful day when I had become extremely exhausted from work and school and got into an argument. Something had to go. It was the stuffed pepper. The pitch, the delivery. WHAM. SLAM. BAM. The Wham and Slam were the pepper hitting its target. The Bam was my dear Italian mother hitting her target: her 4-foot 11 inch frame delivered quite a wallop. It was a crescendo of sound that had my ears ringing.

I loved those peppers so from that day I have never thrown a stuffed pepper at anyone or anything.

For those who prefer eating delicious peperoni imbottiti rather than flinging them, here's the recipe:

> 4 large green peppers
> 4 anchovy filets
> 1 cup Italian bread crumbs. Use stale bread and large crumbs.
>   (Don't use refined commercial crumbs.)
> Cheese, salt, pepper, parsley to taste
> 1 cup tomatoes

Wash peppers and remove stems and seeds, leaving the pepper whole. Combine dry ingredients and stuff peppers. Top each pepper with crust of Italian bread.

If mother didn't have anchovies, she would use Spanish olives or even grape jam as substitutes. Arrange peppers in baking dish, pour olive oil and tomatoes over each and bake in hot oven for about 20 minutes. Serve hot.

cipollini
small onions

This was another favorite of my father. One of the many things my father taught me; compliments will get you almost anything. My father was the master of the compliment. Whenever he had the urge for cipollini he had to request it with style. Cipollini was a luxury and my mother would not tolerate luxury foods when preparing meals. It required extra time in the daily meal preparation. If my father had a craving for those tiny onions he began preparing his request days in advance. We called it "softening up".

"You know what I was thinking of today, Generosa. Maybe it would be nice to add to your delicacy for tomorrow night an added treat to the treat you are already planning... just a small insignificant, but then, nothing you do, no matter how small, is insignificant. How about some cipollini?"

That was called placing a special request. The answer was never immediate. He was kept dangling.

And only during the meal and when the entree was served, did he know whether his request had been accepted. My father was the master of the compliment, but no one could match my mother when it came to being the master of the kitchen.

When the time came to produce the tiny onions she did it with magic. Presto. An inside softball serve and there were the cipollini. The aroma had you salivating.

"Oh, my dear. What a surprise," father would say. "You made them so soon", and before you could utter the word "cipollini" my father began his feast. More bread. A little extra wine. More and more cipollini. We never asked for a serving. We knew it was his treat. The serving was small and we wanted him to enjoy.

To prepare this dish, buy the small onions found in markets which cater to Mediterrean meals.

Peel the onions and wash thoroughly. Cut sharp criss cross slits into each onion. Place the onions in a saucepan and cover with water, bringing the water up to the top. Salt and cook slowly bringing them to a boiling point and continue boiling for 20 minutes.

Remove the onions and fry in olive oil; add garlic and strips of green pepper and saute for 10 minutes. Allow the concoction to cool before serving. You can add some heated tomato sauce to the onions for added flavoring. Serves 3-4, depending on greed.

    1 lb cipollini
    1 tsp salt
    2 tbsp olive oil
    1 clove garlic
    1 green bell pepper

spinacio
spinach

For some peculiar reason spinach was not one of my favorites until that day my father brought me a page from the Newark *Star-Eagle* (now *Star-Ledger*) and showed me drawings which he called cartoona.

"See how strong this sailor is when he eats his spinach" he said, pointing to the character we all now know as Popeye. In one frame Popeye had been bound and gagged by the notorious Bluto who wanted to steal Popeye's girlfriend Olive. I always thought she was an Italian because her name was Olive. In the next frame, Popeye managed to reach into his shirt (how, I don't know) and got a can of spinach. In no time the can was opened, the spinach swallowed and all sorts of power surged through his body. In the next frame Popeye burst from his chains and rescued Olive.

Somehow, that episode thrilled me and I enthusiastically ate my spinach. And whenever I had difficulty eating spinach I would, to get me in the mood, sit down at my little blackboard and draw Popeye. Most kids had small blackboards in those days.

The spinach we ate was prepared with that magic ingredient: olive oil. Thoroughly wash the spinach in salted water until clean. (My mother washed most things in salt water which acted as a cleansing agent.) After the spinach is washed, place it in water that has been brought to a boil. Then add salt, cover the pan and turn off the gas. (Those with an electric range should remove the pan from the heating element.) The spinach is left in the hot water for about two or three minutes. Then remove the spinach from the water and allow it to drain. Don't throw away all the spinach water – you will need it. While the spinach is draining in a colander, prepare the following mixture. Pour three tablespoons of olive oil into the spinach water. Then put in one clove of garlic and a teaspoon of salt and boil mixture over low heat for 15 minutes. Cover the pan while cooking. After the mixture has been cooking for 15 minutes add the spinach and cook for 20 minutes. When that is done, you have a delicious vegetable which can be served with meat or fish. For added pleasure dip some Italian bread in the spinach broth . . . it's delicious.

arrostito peperoni
roasted peppers

One of the side treats my mother made to add flavor to meats, sandwiches or even fish was roasted peppers. This is a very easy dish to make. I remember a time when I was in mid-grade school and my mother was ill with bronchitis. My sister and I were given the job of finishing the roasted peppers. My mother had a flat pan with a grid and cover in which we placed the bell peppers.

My mother wanted to have peppers as a treat for my father. We were also having eggplant and cheese as the main dish. She was able to make the eggplant but didn't feel well enough to continue with the peppers.

Here's that recipe: Simply wash and dry four large green bell peppers and put on a broiler rack. Broil for about 10 minutes. There is no need to cover the peppers as we did on the coal stove. When the outer skin of the peppers look slightly burned remove the peppers from the broiler and peel off the brown skin. Also remove the stems and seeds and tear the peppers into one inch wide strips. Place the peppers in a bowl and when cool add chopped garlic (one clove), salt, two tablespoons of olive oil, stir and serve. Serves four to six.

arrostito castagno
roasted chestnuts

After a satisfying winter meal ranging from pasta to roast chicken we invariably would top the meal with roasted chestnuts and more red wine.

Sometimes it was Dad's job to prepare the chestnuts but not always for he only entered the sanctum santorum by the grace of my dear Italian mother.

The chestnuts are prepared quite easily. First, be certain you get chestnuts which are edible. (Not horse chestnuts as some have done in the past.)

Slit the chestnuts and bake in a 350 degree oven for 20-30 minutes. And that's it. Pour the wine, continue the conversation and peel the chestnuts. All this must be executed with gusto.

peperoni e uova
peppers and eggs

Here is a treat that works to satisfy hunger when you can't think of anything else to prepare. It is a good recipe for a morning brunch and can give you renewed vigor after a long night.

My mother always prepared peppers and eggs whenever she ran out of ideas for lunch. We never had cold cuts in our house so meals weren't easy for mother.

First, dice up a large bell pepper and chop a medium-sized onion. Place together in large frying pan of warming olive oil. You can use peanut or corn oil but I prefer olive oil. Also drop in a clove of garlic and cook the ingredients. When they are well heated, which should take about ten minutes on a medium heat, pour in four eggs which you have scrambled in a separate bowl. Then add salt, black crushed pepper and a few pinches of crushed red pepper. Serve this hot in Italian rolls or with toast. A glass or two of burgundy and you have made the day begin properly. This can serve two or three persons depending how hungry you are. If you want to add some grated cheese while the mixture is cooking, do it. It can add a little flavor. However, no more than a half teaspoon. Eat and enjoy.

cicoria con aglio
dandelions with garlic

Whenever I tell friends I ate dandelions as a child they can't imagine a meal of nasty weeds which grow out of cracks in the sidewalk. Our dandelions, however, were grown with the delicate touch of truck farmers in the famous vegetable farms of the garden state of which Newark is the principal municipality. Ah, yes, those invigorating dandelions which have a bitter taste to them but so nourishing and satisfying that I always felt a surge of new energy whenever I devoured Mom's dandelions with olive oil. She always told us it was good for our skin.

Today, supermarkets in most major cities carry dandelions. You can usually find them in markets which cater to customers well acquainted with all sorts of exotic vegetables, especially those catering to Italian-Americans. The taste is similar to the chicory plant. Dandelions may be served in salads or as a hot dish. I prefer the latter.

Start with about two pounds of cultivated Italian dandelions. These dandelions are not to be confused with the sidewalk variety which has that bright yellow flower. When you get the Italian dandelions, wash and clean thoroughly. Cut the leaves in bite sizes. Cook in boiling water for five minutes.

Heat the olive oil, water, salt and garlic in a saucepan. Add the dandelions. Cook slowly until tender. Serves 4.

2 lbs dandelions
4 tbsp olive oil
2 cloves garlic, chopped
salt to taste
1/2 cup of vegetable water. This is the water in which the
   dandelions were cooked.

uova con acqua e salle
egg with salt and water

I had just finished leaving a trail of flour around the kitchen table when who should walk in. She was furious.

"What are you doing? All the trouble I got and now this." My mother darted at me like a linebacker at Notre Dame. Her brown eyes were wider than usual and I could see vividly that she had mayhem in mind.

"That's alright, Ma. Nothing happened," I said racing around the table as she pursued with her favorite equalizer . . . a long-handled wooden spoon.

"I was only decorating," I said struggling for a good lie. Actually, I was angry about something that had happened and wanted to get even.

"Deck-a-what? Never mind . . ." she gave one large lunge and caught me right at the knees, a handful of knickers in her tight fist. Down I went sliding through the flour and my mother landing smack on top. Wallop! "Ooh, that hurts." Wallop! "Ooh, that hurts more."

"Now, you used all the flour. And I was going to use it for marble cake." (See page 76.) "Wait until your father gets home. You'll get it then," she warned.

"Tonight, just for what you did you will get acqua and salle (salt and water)."

Salt and water may sound like a French Foreign Legion torture. Actually it is egg poached in olive oil and salted water and poured over thick, day-old Italian bread. Today, it's a treat. In the Depression, it meant extra hard times or a mother was taking disciplinary action.

This is how my dear Italian mother made it. Put the required amount of olive oil, water, salt and parsley in a frying pan and bring to a boil. Crack and drop one or two eggs into the boiling water and poach. Cook until the egg is well done, basting often.

Place two thick slices of Italian bread in a soup plate. Sprinkle bread with grated cheese. Then remove poached egg or eggs from water and put on bread. Then pour the boiling liquid over the egg and bread. Enjoy. A glass of red dry wine and you will forget all your beatings. Serves 2.

This is the recipe:
>   1 tbsp olive oil
>   1/2 cup water
>   salt to taste
>   parsley (several sprigs)
>   romano cheese
>   one or two eggs

72

salada pomodoro

tomato salad

Italian salad sometimes leaves you wanting more. However, the simplicity can be rewarding when you accompany the salad with a spicy entree such as breaded veal cutlet or stew.

My mother prepared a very plain tomato salad but it always worked with her meals. Simply, she used four fresh garden tomatoes (medium sized) and seasoning. Wash the tomatoes and slice. Then add salt, pepper, garlic (chopped) and oregano. Pour olive oil over the tomatoes and chill before serving. This makes a refreshing salad during the hot summer months.

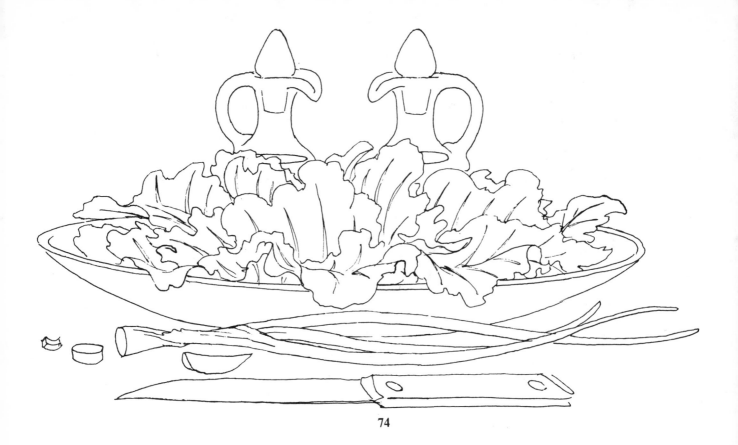

74

salada con escarole
escarole salad

Few restaurants serve escarole salad, partly because few markets even sell the green. However, if you are fortunate enough to locate an outlet you can have a refreshing salad for the summer months. Take one head of escarole and prepare it for salad by pulling it apart – not cutting it. Add to this a chopped small onion and season with salt, pepper, chopped garlic, oregano, wine vinegar and olive oil. Mix to taste. Don't overdo it with the vinegar – about a teaspoon will do. Escarole also makes a great hot dish. (See page 44.)

dolce mai morato

marblecake

While this did not come from the shores of Guardia Lombardy, it is part of my memories of my dear Italian mother. It was her specialty, something that she gleaned from old Italian recipes and which was a favorite of many in our neighborhood. It was the prize we sought if we were good. However, if we failed to meet her expectations we generally had to use other means such as waking up during the middle of the night and sneaking into the kitchen.

I can remember that one night. The kitchen was dark. There was little light coming from the night outside and I could barely see ahead. However, I knew where my mother kept it. I felt for the cabinet doors and slowly began opening them. I poked around inside. I felt it. It was in a round metal can. My mother had failed again to hide her favorite marble cake from me.

We were only given cake after dinner, never between meals. But I was a cake freak and had to have the marble cake. The knives were nearby and it didn't take too long to cut myself a chunk of that delicious cake.

The next day my mother discovered the theft and surprisingly was not angry. She did warn me that someday, "You like cake so much, you will marry for a cake." Not exactly, but my dear wife was a cook par excellence.

Here are the ingredients:

    1/4 lb butter
    1 full cup of sugar
    3 eggs
    2-1/2 cups of flour
    2-1/2 tsp of baking powder
    1 tsp vanilla
    2 or 3 tsp of Nestle's or Hershey's cocoa
    1 tsp of lemon extract
    1 cup milk

Cream the butter, mixing in the sugar and vanilla. Add to this mixture the eggs which have been beaten separately. Then add milk, the flour which has been sifted and the baking powder. Beat well. Three hundred strokes will do.

Remove about 6 tablespoons of the mixture and place in a separate bowl. Now add the cocoa and lemon extract to the bowl containing the smaller of the mixture. Pour 1/2 of the white batter into a well greased round 2" or more high baking pan. Now add the chocolate batter to the white batter. Zigzag the chocolate batter through the white batter using a spatula. When that is done add the remaining white batter. Bake at 350 degrees for about 45 minutes.

Now that I have shared some of these recipes, you can better understand my total allegiance to the art of Italian peasant cooking.

What joy this will bring to you and your loved ones and the friends and acquaintances you might wish to have at your table.

Consider this: when you cook these foods they are not a scientific creation of some test tube jockey but foods whose recipes have been prepared with love and feeling that transcends not only several generations but thousands of miles of ocean.

They came from the tiny hamlets that were home to Italians who tilled and toiled the rocky high ground of the mountainous regions of Campagna. When they prepared these foods, they did it with love, as did my mother.

To these people, and more particularly my dear mother, I express my deepest thanks and gratitude. Had it not been for her perseverance and her devotion, the joy of Italian food may not have remained with me all these years.

My only wish is that I have successfully transmitted the recipes as well as the loving care which she put into each dish, be it the elegant linguine con aglio e olio di oliva or the just plain, but, oh so delicious pasta e fagioli.

Thank you, Ma.

Appendix

Now, what you may have read about Italians and family may sound romantic but subtract the Latin myth about cohesiveness and they are no different from any other ethnic group. Except, of course, in one small, significant way: food.

In this whole world there is absolutely nothing that compares with the aroma coming from an Italian kitchen. Spoil yourself for a minute and visualize linguine sauted in olive oil and garlic with a few sprigs of parsley and accompanied by freshly-cut mushrooms. My senses overtake me as I try to convey the rapture that comes over me when I sit down to an authentic Italian meal prepared the Neopolitan way.

These additional recipes have been handed down from generation to generation in a small community in the region of Campania where is located, the city of Naples, the capital seat of all Italian cooking. Beyond this region Italian cooking is noteworthy, but I can not, in all honesty give it the same respect I give Neopolitan cooking.

In my family, small though it be, conversation always returns to : "What did you have for dinner?"

Never mind that conversation may have been detoured from an exciting discussion on politics or sibling rivalry. When it focused on what we had eaten or planned to eat, our rationality was dismissed and our emotions took over.

CAVOLO CON OLIO di OLIVA
(green) cabbage with olive oil

Ingredients

two (2) lbs green cabbage
two (2) tbsps olive oil
two (2) cloves of garlic
three (3) strips of bacon (uncut)

Prepare your cabbage by removing leaves, washing them
and placing the entire serving in a large pan of water. Bring
to a boil and cook until tender. Drain

In another pot or the pot in which the cabbage was cooked
pour in olive oil and shelled, crushed cloves of garlic and
place in the strips of bacon. Cook until bacon is crisp and
then put in the drained cabbage and allow to simmer for
several minutes. Salt and pepper to taste. Serve hot. Excellent winter dish accompanied by Italian or French bread
and of course, a glass of dry red wine.

Makes four servings

CAVOLFIORE O BROCCOLI (dorito e frito)
cauliflower or broccolo (dipped and fried)

Ingredients

one small head of cauliflower or broccoli
three tbsp corn or olive oil
one half-cup of flour
two eggs
salt, pepper, oregano
two tbsp of freshly chopped parsley
two tbsp. grated cheese (Romano or Parmesan)

Wash vegetables thoroughly and cut into small stalks
containing a bud of the flower. Prepare two small bowls.
One containing flour seasoned with salt, pepper and oregano; the other, with beaten eggs seasoned with grated
cheese and chopped fresh parsley. Dip stalks into beaten
eggs seasoned with grated cheese and chopped fresh parsley. Then dip and coat with flour. Saute in a shallow pan
until toasty brown and serve hot. Excellent to serve as
appetizer or with main course. A light red wine, preferably Chianti, would add zest to the meal. For a light lunch
serve the above with a provolone or gorganzola cheese,
and appropreiate bread.

makes two servings

SCAMORZA (mozarella) EN CAROZZA
or Cheese in a Carriage

Ingredients

one lb. mozarella, sliced medium thin
eight slices white bread
three eggs
one-eighth cup of milk
salt, pepper
two tbsps olive oil
chopped parsley (fresh or dried)

In a bowl combine eggs and milk and whisk vigorously with fork. Add salt and pepper eggs to taste. Add a pinch of parsley. Dip slices of bread one at a time into the bowl containing the beaten eggs and milk. Meantime, heat olive oil over medium flame or heat. Place the two slices into frying pan. When the slices are slighlty golden, place slices of mozarella on one slice and cover with the other. (You are making a toasted cheese sandwich) Flip over several times until cheese is melted. Repeat process. Serve hot. Accompany with green salad and red or white table wine.

makes four servings

ZUCCHINE CON OLIO E POMODORI
zucchini with oil and tomatoes

Ingredients

one cup of canned tomatoes, strained
one-half green bell pepper, cut in strips
Three (3) small zucchini (about two pounds) cut in chunks
two cloves of garlic, peeled
Romano or Parmesan cheese, grated
one egg
fresh or dried parsley
salt, pepper, oregano
red wine (optional)

In a sauce pan combine peeled garlic, bell pepper cut into strips. Saute in three tablespoons of olive oil for several minutes over low heat. Add zucchini unpeeled and cut into chunks and strained tomatoes. Allow to cook over low heat for about 30 minutes. Add salt, pepper and oregano to taste. Add beaten egg and one teaspoon grated cheese. For added flavor, add an ounce of red wine. Serve with Italian or French bread and a light red wine. Ideal for autumn lunch. Dessert: fresh fruit or a sweet something, accompanied by coffee.

makes two servings

PIZZA FRITO DOLCE (fried sweet pizza)

Ingredients
one-half lb pizza dough
two tbsp sugar
corn oil

(see pizza dough recipe for preparing pizza dough, on reverse side)

Make several palm-sized patties of pizza dough about one inch thick and saute in a pan containing corn oil. Saute patties until light brown or done to your taste. Remove patties from pan and sprinkle with sugar. Serve warm. Excellent cold weather breakfast-treat. Accompany with latte or espresso or, if you must, milk.

(This recipe was originally a recipe from my paternal grandmother handed down to me from my father who now denies he ever had a sweet tooth.)

Makes four small pizzas

pizza dough

Ingredients

three and one-half cups of sifted flour
one tsp (leveled) salt
two packages dry yeast
one and one-quater cups of luke warm water
pinch of sugar

Sprinkle yeast and sugar into one-quarter cup of luke warm water, stir and let stand for several minutes until the yeast bubbles and mixture increases in size. If yeast does not bubble start process again with fresh yeast.

Into large bowl, pour in sifted flour and salt and yeast mixture, adding one cup of luke warm water. Stir vigorously by hand or with electric mixer. When dough becomes a rough mixture, remove and place on floured board and knead it for about 15 minutes, or until it is smooth and elastic. Then dust the mixture lightly with flour and let rise about two hours or until double in bulk. Then place again on floured board and knead lightly to deflate. Divide into pieces. Dough may be prepared in the above manner or purchased from a baker or use prepared pizza dough mix.

makes four servings